BIBLE

MISFITERS AND VILLAINS

GARRETT ROMINES AND CHRISTOPHER MIKO

STORIES FROM THE BIBLE
TOLD BLOCK BY BLOCK

LION

Text copyright © 2016 Christopher Miko and Garrett Romines
Illustrations copyright © 2016 Christopher Miko and Garrett Romines
This mini edition copyright © 2017 Lion Hudson

The right of Christopher Miko and Garrett Romines to be identified as the authors and illustrators of this work has been asserted by them in accordance with the Copyright, Designs and Patents Act 1988.

Published by Lion Books
an imprint of
Lion Hudson plc
Wilkinson House, Jordan Hill Road,
Oxford OX2 8DR, England
www.lionhudson.com/lion

ISBN 978 0 7459 7730 0

Original Bible edition published by Sky Pony Press, 307 West 36th Street, 11th Floor, New York, NY 10018

Stories originally published in *The Unofficial Old Testament for Minecrafters* and *The Unofficial New Testament for Minecrafters* 2016
This mini edition 2017

Acknowledgments
A catalogue record for this book is available from the British Library
Minecraft ® is a registered trademark of Notch Development AB.
The Minecraft ® game is copyright © Mojang AB.

Printed and bound in China, February 2017, LH41

CONTENTS

FOREWORD

I'm always on the lookout for new ways to tell Bible stories. That's what storytellers do. The hardest job is finding a compelling and original "way in" to a story. And when I find something that works, I get really excited.

A few years back, the publishers behind the original US edition of these books created *The Brick Bible*. My son immediately went out and bought a copy. So OK, he's 33, but he's a LEGO ® fanatic, and he thought that the idea was absolutely brilliant!

He may not be quite so keen on Minecraft ®, but my grandchildren are. They don't get much game-playing time, but when they do, Minecraft ® is their first choice. The older two (nine and six) love building the worlds, while the youngest, who is only three, simply enjoys digging holes and getting stuck in them.

So when I showed them a few sample pages from *The Unofficial Bible for Minecrafters*, they got the same look on their faces that my son had on his when he found *The Brick Bible*. Their responses ranged from "It's funny" (which it is!) to "When can I read some more?"

As for me, I turned the pages just to see what the creators of the book would get up to next and how they would bring each scene to Minecrafter-life. And I have to say that I was surprised and delighted.

Every now and then, someone comes up with a new way of telling Bible stories that is just that little bit different. And if this is a "way in" for someone (and there are thousands of Minecrafters out there) and it's compelling, intriguing, and faithful to the text, then I'm happy to recommend it. That's what storytellers do.

Bob Hartman

Bob Hartman, Storyteller

CAIN AND ABEL
Genesis 4

Oh dear, Gabriel.

What's the matter, Lord?

I wanted everything to be beautiful and good, but it hasn't turned out that way. And now I foresee trouble.

ADAM AND EVE SETTLED OUTSIDE THE GARDEN OF EDEN. THEY HAD TWO SONS: CAIN AND ABEL.

ABEL'S JOB WAS TO CARE FOR THE FLOCKS.

AND CAIN TOOK CARE OF THE SOIL.

My sons, let us make offerings to God to show our thanks for all that he gives us.

I cannot wait to give thanks to God. I will give him plenty!

The time has come for us to give our share.

I will give very little!

CAIN BROUGHT SOME LEFTOVERS FROM HIS HARVEST.

GOD WAS PLEASED WITH ABEL, BUT NOT WITH CAIN.

ABEL BROUGHT A LAMB, THE BEST OF HIS FLOCK.

3

God will never know what I have done!

Cain! Where is your brother?

BUT GOD SEES EVERYTHING, AND HE CALLED OUT TO CAIN.

I don't know. Am I my brother's keeper?

What have you done? Your brother's blood cries out to me. You are now cursed, and can no longer farm the soil. The earth will yield no crops for you. You will wander this world until you die.

Please God, this punishment is more than I can take.

MOSES AND PHARAOH
Exodus 5–12

I have a feeling this doesn't bode well for the Egyptians.

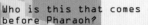

Who is this that comes before Pharaoh?

It is I, Moses. I have a message for you from the God of the Israelites. He says this: "Let my people go!"

THE ISRAELITE LEADER, MOSES, WENT BEFORE PHARAOH TO SPEAK FOR GOD'S PEOPLE WHO WERE BEING FORCED TO WORK AS SLAVES IN EGYPT. HE STOOD TALL AND BRAVE.

I am Pharaoh of Egypt, a living god on Earth, and I will bow to no one!

Teach these Israelites a lesson — work them harder! I will show them who their master is.

Yes, Your Majesty.

PHARAOH WAS DETERMINED TO SHOW MOSES WHO WAS IN CHARGE. THINGS GOT MUCH WORSE FOR THE ISRAELITES.

MOSES SPOKE TO PHARAOH ON THE BANKS OF THE RIVER NILE.

MOSES TOUCHED THE WATER WITH HIS STAFF AND THE WATER TURNED TO BLOOD.

NEXT PHARAOH LOOKED OUTSIDE AND SAW THAT ALL OF EGYPT WAS COVERED IN FROGS.
This cannot be happening. Curse this God of Moses! Doesn't he know who he is dealing with? I will never bend to his will!

NEXT, GOD SENT A PLAGUE OF GNATS ONTO THE LAND, AND AGAIN PHARAOH REFUSED TO LET THE ISRAELITES GO. SO THEN GOD SENT SWARMS OF FLIES.

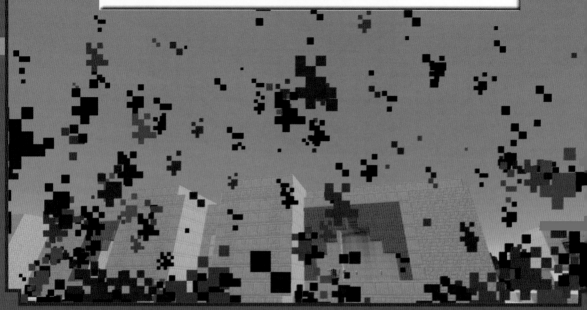

PHARAOH STILL DID NOT GIVE IN, SO GOD SENT PLAGUES OF DISEASE TO KILL THE ANIMALS, BOILS, AND HAIL. FINALLY, A PLAGUE OF LOCUSTS ATE ALL THAT WAS GREEN ON THE LAND, AND PLUNGED EGYPT INTO FAMINE.

GOD THEN COVERED THE LAND IN DARKNESS FOR THREE DAYS TO WARN PHARAOH THAT HE MUST RELEASE THE ISRAELITES. BUT PHARAOH STILL WOULD NOT LET THEM GO.

SO CAME THE TENTH AND FINAL PLAGUE. GOD TOLD THE ISRAELITES TO PLACE LAMB'S BLOOD ON THEIR DOORPOSTS THAT NIGHT. THIS WOULD SHOW THE ANGEL OF DEATH WHICH HOUSEHOLDS TO SPARE.

AS THE ANGEL OF DEATH PASSED OVER EACH HOUSE THAT WAS MARKED WITH LAMB'S BLOOD, THIS BECAME KNOWN AS THE PASSOVER.

AND SO IT WAS THAT THE ANGEL OF DEATH PASSED BY THE DOORS OF THE ISRAELITES, BUT STRUCK DOWN THE FIRSTBORN CHILDREN OF ALL THE OTHER FAMILIES IN EGYPT, INCLUDING THAT OF PHARAOH.

THAT NIGHT PHARAOH SUMMONED MOSES. IT WAS CLEAR THAT PHARAOH HAD HAD A CHANGE OF HEART.

Get out, and take your people with you!

FINALLY FREE, THE ISRAELITES HASTILY SET OUT WITH MOSES TO THE LAND THAT GOD HAD PROMISED THEM.

SAMSON AND DELILAH

Judges 16

I think this man's
will cause him more
good.

Your hair is so beautiful.

So is yours!

SAMSON THE STRONG FELL IN LOVE WITH A WOMAN NAMED DELILAH.

THE RULERS OF THE PHILISTINES FEARED AND HATED SAMSON. THEY MET TO DISCUSS HOW TO DEAL WITH HIM.

There must be a way to overpower him.

He is unstoppable.

How do we do that?

Samson must have a weakness. We just need to find out what it is.

We will pay a woman to find out and she will tell us.

I know the exact person: a woman named Delilah. I'm sure she'll do it for a big enough reward.

SHE LET THE PHILISTINES ENTER THE HOUSE.

He is in here.

WHILE SAMSON SLEPT, THEY CUT HIS HAIR.

We have you now.

WHEN HE AWOKE, THE PHILISTINES SEIZED HIM. SAMSON TRIED TO STRUGGLE FREE BUT HE WAS AS WEAK AS A BABY.

SAMSON WAS TAKEN TO PRISON, WHERE HE AWAITED HIS PUNISHMENT. HERE HIS CAPTORS PUT OUT HIS EYES. NOW SAMSON WAS BLIND.

SOON, THE PHILISTINES SENT HIM TO THE PRISON MILL TO GRIND GRAIN.

DELILAH RETURNED TO THE PHILISTINE RULERS TO RECEIVE HER REWARD.

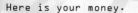

Here is your money.

I'm rich!

SAMSON REMAINED IN PRISON, BUT SLOWLY THE HAIR ON HIS HEAD BEGAN TO GROW BACK.

ONE DAY, IN THE TEMPLE, THE PHILISTINES GATHERED FOR A GREAT CELEBRATION.

WHILE THE CROWD WAS IN HIGH SPIRITS, THEY SHOUTED FOR SAMSON.

Bring out Samson!

SAMSON WAS BROUGHT BEFORE THE CROWD.
Welcome, Samson! Perhaps you can perform a few tricks for our entertainment.
Behold the once mighty Samson!
EVERYONE LAUGHED TO SEE SAMSON IN CHAINS.
Boy, put me where I can feel the pillars that hold up the temple.
They are here.
SINCE HE WAS UNABLE TO SEE, SAMSON RELIED UPON A YOUNG BOY TO HELP HIM.
Now, my child, RUN!

SAMSON REACHED FOR THE PILLARS AND PRAYED TO GOD.

Lord, please grant my strength just once more, so that I can get even with the Philistines.

THEN GOD'S MIGHTY POWER CAME OVER SAMSON. HE PUSHED AGAINST THE PILLARS WITH ALL HIS MIGHT AND THE TEMPLE CAME DOWN, KILLING EVERYONE INSIDE, INCLUDING HIMSELF.

23

DAVID AND GOLIATH
1 Samuel 17

It's time the people of Israel were shown that faith is stronger than brawn.

THE PEOPLE OF ISRAEL WERE ALWAYS FIGHTING THEIR NEIGHBOURS, THE PHILISTINES. ONCE AGAIN, THE PHILISTINES ATTACKED. ALL THE MEN OF ISRAEL WERE CALLED TO SERVE IN THE ARMY.

THE TWO ARMIES HELD THEIR GROUND ON OPPOSITE SIDES OF A DRY RIVERBED.

IT WAS THE CUSTOM FOR EACH SIDE TO CHOOSE A CHAMPION TO FIGHT EACH OTHER. THE ARMY OF THE DEFEATED CHAMPION WOULD THEN SURRENDER.

25

FOR FORTY DAYS GOLIATH WAITED FOR AN ISRAELITE TO STEP FORWARD. THEN ONE DAY, DAVID WENT TO THE FRONT LINE.

HE SPOKE TO KING SAUL.

You are only a boy, and Goliath has been a warrior for many years.

I have killed lions and bears with only a sling. With God's help, I will win this battle.

DAVID WAS NOT SCARED OF GOLIATH. GOLIATH MOVED TOWARD DAVID.

DAVID FITTED A STONE IN HIS SLING. IT FLEW THROUGH THE AIR AND STRUCK GOLIATH ON THE FOREHEAD.

THE GIANT FELL TO THE GROUND, DEAD.

We're doomed. Run!

WHEN THE PHILISTINES SAW GOLIATH FALL,
THEY TURNED AND RAN IN HORROR.

THEY TRIED TO ESCAPE FROM THE ISRAELITES.

BUT THE ISRAELITES PURSUED THEM AND WERE VICTORIOUS THAT DAY.

JESUS AND THE PHARISEES

Matthew 12; Mark 3;
Luke 6

According to Moses, Jesus isn't allowed to heal people on the sabbath... I think he's going to get into trouble.

ONE DAY WHILE JESUS PREACHED, A MAN WITH A PARALYSED HAND CAME UP TO HIM.

Look! A man with a paralysed hand. Let's see if Jesus will heal him on the sabbath.

If he does, we can accuse him of breaking the laws of Moses.

THE PHARISEES, WHO WERE JEWISH LEADERS, WATCHED CLOSELY TO SEE WHAT JESUS WOULD DO. THEY WERE ALWAYS LOOKING FOR A REASON TO ACCUSE HIM.

That's it - stand up there so that everyone can see you.

JESUS KNEW WHAT THEY WERE THINKING AND CALLED ON THE MAN TO STAND UP AT THE FRONT.

THEN JESUS TURNED TO THE CROWD.

I have a question for you. What does the law let us do on the sabbath: good or harm? Are we allowed to save life or should we kill?

EVERYONE WAS SILENT.

JESUS LOOKED SADLY AROUND HIM, SEEING THE PEOPLE'S INDIGNATION AND FURY. THEN HE SPOKE TO THE MAN WITH THE PARALYSED HAND.

Stretch out your hand.

THE MAN STRETCHED OUT HIS HAND, AND IMMEDIATELY IT WAS HEALED.

That is it! We must stop him!

We mustn't just stop him. That man needs to be got rid of, once and for all.

THE PHARISEES WERE FILLED WITH RAGE, AND SET OUT TO PLOT AGAINST JESUS.

PETER AND THE ELDERS
Acts 3–4

Jesus has gone to heaven, but his right-hand man continues to spread God's message.

ONE DAY, THE DISCIPLES PETER AND JOHN WERE GOING UP TO THE TEMPLE TO PRAY.

WHEN THE MAN SAW PETER AND JOHN, HE CALLED OUT.

Please can you spare a coin or two?

NEAR ONE OF THE TEMPLE GATES LAY A MAN WHO WAS UNABLE TO WALK.

PETER LOOKED AT HIM AND REPLIED GENTLY.

I have neither silver nor gold, but what I do have I will give you.

THEN HE STRETCHED OUT HIS HAND TOWARD THE MAN AND ORDERED HIM TO STAND UP AND WALK.

In the name of Jesus Christ, walk!

I'm walking! I'm walking!

STRENGTH SURGED INTO THE MAN'S LIMBS. HE LEAPED TO HIS FEET, AND INSTANTLY BEGAN TO WALK.

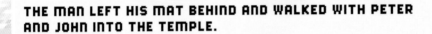

THE MAN LEFT HIS MAT BEHIND AND WALKED WITH PETER AND JOHN INTO THE TEMPLE.

WHEN THE PEOPLE SAW HIM WALKING AND PRAISED GOD, THEY WERE FILLED WITH WONDER.

Praise be to God!

How?

I don't understand.

PETER APPROACHED AN ONLOOKER.

What's the matter? Why are you so surprised?

THE PEOPLE RAN UP TO THE DISCIPLES.

Why do you keep staring at us? It wasn't our power that made this man walk.

PETER ADDRESSED THEM.

The God of Abraham, Isaac, and Jacob, the God of our ancestors, has given his divine glory to servant Jesus.

This man, who was unable to walk, was made strong. It was faith in Jesus that healed him.

Now is the time to be sorry and to turn to God, so that he will forgive your sins... The covenant God made with your ancestors was also for you... and God sent his servant Jesus to you so that you could give up the bad things in your lives and come back to God.

MANY PEOPLE BECAME FOLLOWERS OF JESUS THAT DAY.

NOW THE PRIESTS AND THE ELDERS HAD COME TO LISTEN TO PETER AND JOHN.

Agreed.

We cannot let this be talked about.

THEY WERE GREATLY DISTURBED THAT THE DISCIPLES WERE TELLING PEOPLE ABOUT JESUS' RESURRECTION.

THEY ORDERED PETER AND JOHN TO BE SEIZED AND PUT IN JAIL.

41

THE NEXT DAY, THE ELDERS AND THE TEACHERS OF THE LAW MET TO DISCUSS WHAT SHOULD HAPPEN TO PETER AND JOHN.

THE DISCIPLES WERE BROUGHT OUT FOR QUESTIONING.

By what power or in whose name did you perform this miracle?

You should all know that it was by the power of the name of Jesus Christ, whom you crucified, and whom God raised from the dead, that this man was healed!

PETER WAS FILLED WITH THE HOLY SPIRIT.

The Scriptures are talking about Jesus when they say: "The stone that you builders rejected has turned out to be the most important stone of all." And we can only be saved through him.

THE ELDERS AND PRIESTS WERE ASTONISHED AT HOW BOLD PETER AND JOHN WERE, AND IT BECAME CLEAR THAT THEY HAD BEEN FRIENDS OF JESUS.

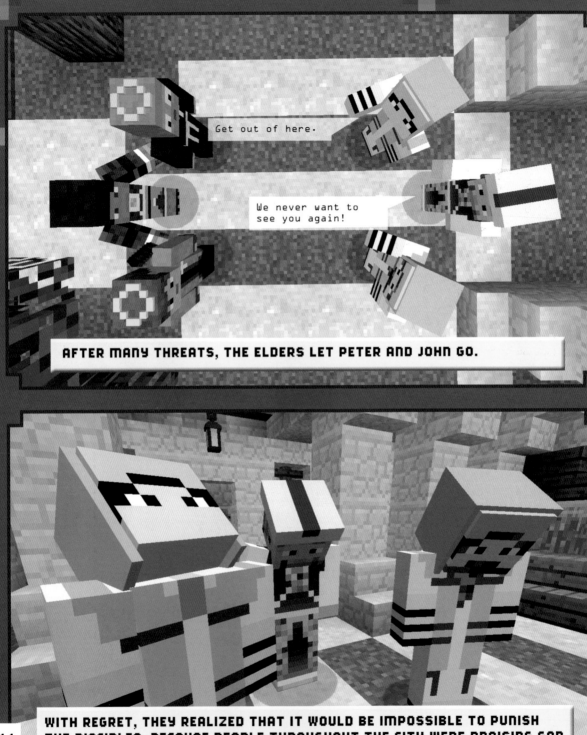

Get out of here.

We never want to see you again!

AFTER MANY THREATS, THE ELDERS LET PETER AND JOHN GO.

WITH REGRET, THEY REALIZED THAT IT WOULD BE IMPOSSIBLE TO PUNISH THE DISCIPLES, BECAUSE PEOPLE THROUGHOUT THE CITY WERE PRAISING GOD FOR WHAT HAD HAPPENED. PETER CONTINUED TO SPREAD JESUS' MESSAGE.